Shellback

JEANNE-MARIE OSTERMAN

Paloma Press, 2021

ISBN 978-1-7344965-3-6

Library of Congress Control Number: 2020935102

Book Design by C. Sophia Ibardaloza

PALOMA PRESS
San Mateo & Morgan Hill, California
Publishing Poetry+Prose since 2016
www.palomapress.net

Acknowledgments

Deep gratitude to the editors of the following journals in which these poems first appeared, sometimes in earlier versions:

45th Parallel: "Any Fool Can"

Aperçus: "Bikini Express," "The Living Will Always Leave You. The Dead Stay with You Forever."

Bluestem: "The String"

Borderlands: "Fukuryu"

Cathexis Northwest: "Rains of Yesteryear," "End Like a Sponge," "Portrait of My Father as a Dad," "On the Stillaguamish River"

The Esthetic Apostle: "That Final Wisdom"

The Madison Review: "Horny Goat Weed"

"Canyon Creek Logging," "Theater of War," and "Horny Goat Weed" appeared in my chapbook, *There's a Hum* (Finishing Line Press, 2018).

For their caring responses to this book in manuscript, I am grateful to Matthew Lippman and Maggie Smith. Thank you to Maria Vargas DeStefano, Martha Savitzky, and Christopher X. Shade for their kindness and friendship. Huge thanks to Aileen Cassinetto of Paloma Press for believing in my work. Above all, love and thanks to my husband, Harold.

For my father,

John D. Osterman

"JDO"

1919 - 2017

Contents

❧

�֎ ✖ ✖

Shellback — 1. An old or veteran sailor. 2. A person who has crossed the equator and been initiated in the traditional ceremony. *(Merriam Webster)*

While the shellback ceremony for U.S. Navy sailors is now a voluntary, morale-boosting celebration, as late as World War II it could take the form of a brutal hazing. This could include beatings with wet firehoses, burial in ship's garbage, and jolts with electrical rods. Some World War II Navy war logs record sailors having to be sent to sick bay after these line crossing initiations.

EPILOGUE

He's losing his grip.
Last Saturday night,
trying to shave for church,
my father cut his face so deep
it bled till 2 AM.
He couldn't reach the Band-Aids
to stanch the blood.
He fell down trying.
He wouldn't ring for help.
He didn't make church.
He won't wear his hearing aid,
so I shout the small talk—
think it'll rain today?
He won't wear a coat
when I take him out
but keeps his thermostat at 88.
He won't open his drapes to see
the view we pay extra for.
I crack them a bit so I can see
to shave his head.
Close those back up,
he says when I finish.
Then he tells me to take down
the poetry book and read
The Cremation of Sam McGee.
I shout all 68 lines
of *that night on the marge*
of Lake Labarge when Cap
cremates his pal Sam.
This is how we talk about death:
He asks me to read
the last part twice
where Sam's frozen corpse
comes back to life.

CANYON CREEK LOGGING, 1937

In a handwritten letter, he tells me how it was
reeling in the moss-covered giants.
We didn't have roads or trucks out there.
We pulled the big cedars in by hand.

With a two-man handsaw the fallers fell the tree.
Choker-man sets hooks deep into the bark
then nods to the whistle punk
to yank the wire
that signals the yarder man
to fire up the steam donkey
that cranks the rig
that pulls the mainline
that hauls her in.

An 11 x 17 Xerox of one of the felled behemoths is attached.
The men perched on top look like ants.
My dad, third from the left, is only 18.
No lights, no phone, no hardhats, he's scrawled on the back.
The water was cold and piped from streams.

OURS WAS A DIVIDED TOWN

On Bayside, the rich.
On Riverside, the poor.
On Bayside, the alleys were paved.
On Riverside, they were tamped down
with slag from the Monte Cristo mines.

> *Those alleys were so full of minerals*
> *they glowed,* my father tells me.
> *I collected it and played with it.*
> *I thought it was pretty.*

The slag's been dredged up and carted away.
The mines are a ghost town now.
The forests have been clear-cut
causing mudslides, causing
whole towns
to disappear.

But right now, we're in that Riverside alley.
I see the blue-green chunks of rock,
the glint in a boy's eye.
It's the height of the Great Depression.
In patched overalls and moth-eaten cap,
he pockets what was once part of a mountain.

HIS THIRD GIRL

I was my father's third girl.
Sundays I tried to be his boy.
I'd lie on the floor at his feet
in front of the Philco.
He'd sit on the naugahyde couch
holding an Oly, explaining
the fair catch, when to punt,
the Hail Mary—what he'd tell his boy
if he had one. I liked watching
the men hitch up their pants
and line up at scrimmage.
I liked the way the quarterback
cupped his hands along
the center's crotch
and grasped the oval ball.
When he fired it at me,
I'd pull that sucker from the air
and run like hell. It got the dog
to barking and my father
so excited, he'd tip over his Oly
on his way to the end zone
to give me the high five.
As he yelled at the screen,
I yelled too, thinking
I was no longer too young,
too dumb, just a girl. Thinking,
of a Sunday, I was his person.

RAINS OF YESTERYEAR

After Gerald Stern's Les Neiges d'Antan

Where did you go, JDO,
in your rag of a shirt and oil-stained pants,
out back of our house on Rainier,
another rainy Saturday,
heaving mildewed magazines,
warped boards, my busted-up high chair
into the flatbed trailer?
I'm there now,
shivering in the damp,
watching you hitch the load
to our '48 four-door Ford—
my day to go to the dump with Daddy,
my job making sure the tongue coupler
stays hooked to the ball as we bounce
over the railroad tracks
and broken streets of Riverside.
I can see you now, ferrying
the load through the mud
to a mountain of trash
that won't burn clean
for the constant drizzle.
I see you hurl in the big pieces,
then shovel the dregs.
I hear you say, *By dusk,*
this'll be a moving carpet of rats,
not afraid I'd be afraid.

'57 OLDS

I'm in the backseat.
JDO's in the driver's seat,
tapping his Old Gold on the dash.
Rain, same as air here,
taps on the roof.
We're watching the people go by.
JDO lights up and blows the smoke slow
like he doesn't care if he clears it all
out of his lungs or not.
Then he turns to me
and says, *When you see someone*
walking down the street,
you have no idea what kind
of personal hell they're in.
I'm nine. My daddy said hell.
I roll down my window
to clear the mist—I want to see
what's far from heaven.

ON THE STILLAGUAMISH RIVER

What was it made me dream so big—
that I could get you to take me down the Stillie,

old rubber raft hanging limp in the basement,
deflated, you not one for water songs?

Why'd you say yes? Hunt down pump and patches,
dry red hands making the bark river-worthy

on the muddy shore? Not my plan to discover anything
out there. I just wanted to take up your time, see how

you, once a sailor, would row, save me from drowning
if I fell in. Yet once underway, I didn't look at you,

or the water. I was fixated on the backs of shacks we passed—
their sagging porches and rickety stairs—

trying to imagine what dramas played out inside.
We passed an old juke joint, empties overflowing

a rusty barrel. Barkeep tossed a tub of ice out the back.
You waved him a buck. *Sell me an Oly?*

Ballast, I stayed low while the can was passed.
I'd have gladly drowned that day.

END LIKE A SPONGE

Kerama Retto, Okinawa, Japan
March 27, 1945

A Japanese pilot breaks through the picket
and crashes on my father's ship.
The pilot pops out of the cockpit,
bounces down the deck.

He's just a torso—
the end like a sponge
filled with blood. It's the sea.
Something in the sea is calling us back to be
the watery creatures we once were—
big-mouthed and baglike,
happy to engulf our food all day.
Then came suicide pilots
and battleships, guns
as long as the Doug firs that line I-5.

Eleven killed plus the pilot.
Missed my father by twenty feet.

The sea, the sea,
we all come from the sea.

The sailors wrap the torso in canvas.
With no limbs or skull,
he's nearly square—
a bag of cement.

They say a prayer and lower him
into the sea. My father,
remembering trees,
doesn't know why he's alive.

WING AND A PRAYER

6:45 AM call to battle stations.
Japanese plane coming straight at them.
Every gun they have begins to fire.
The gunners tear off a wing.
A few sailors join hands and hold a prayer meeting.
The burning wing cartwheels
through the air and hits the turret,
killing the gunners who shot it off.
Sailors lie among burning metal—
some missing heads, limbs. Some still moving,
alive, crisp black hands holding
imaginary guns.

THEATER OF WAR

Here's how it looked after the kamikaze hit,
my father says, holding the cruise book in his lap.

The Japanese plane looks like a ball
of crumpled paper on the ship's massive deck.

Next to the wreckage, eleven mummies
wrapped in white canvas and the American flag.

KEEP OFF is written in white chalk along their feet.
One at a time we put them on a table. We used

a mess hall table. We weighted each man
with a cannon ball and tipped him into the sea.

FUKURYU

Term used by the Japanese for suicide swimmers, the "unsung kamikazes," who swam underwater to U.S. ships, chained themselves to the hull and detonated the bombs they carried on bamboo poles.

You turn yourself into a fish.
Your teeth, a bomb on a bamboo pole.
Your sacred scarf flutters behind you,
an angelfish fin. No ifs:
your death guaranteed
when you detonate.
Mine chain! a sailor shouts,
hearing your rattle against the hull.
You're caught in a net
and hoisted aboard,
your dream of dying ending
in life, the sailors too shocked
by your small size to celebrate.
You are all teenagers.

ON THE USS NEVADA

We each had an interesting job,
my father tells me over a bowl of chili.
The powder man lifted the powder case onto the gun's rammer tray.
The projectile man pulled the rammer lever that loaded the chamber.
The check sight made sure we were aimed at the target.
The hot case man caught the shells that flew from the guns.

Those shells were the size of a little league bat, he says,
making fists as if holding a slugger.
He threw them into a tub of seawater,
and when the guns weren't blasting, you could hear them sizzle.

He sets down his spoon and wipes his mouth.
My job, he says, *didn't have a name.*

I went through the stuff of the guys who got killed.
I separated it into two piles:
one of any items like letters or pictures
that might be offensive to wives or parents.

The rest was shipped back home.

THINK OF IT

April 1, 1945. Easter Sunday. First day of the battle of Okinawa in which 50,000 Americans and 100,000 Japanese were killed.

Think of an island,
a rocky coast,
some caves.

Winding roads,
thatched-roof huts,
umbrella trees.

A line of ships,
guns pointing
like fingers.

Spotter planes
buzzing like flies
over a supper plate.

Ships giving birth—
landing tanks tumbling
from the monster hole,
scuttling to shore.

The rocky coast
pounded to powder,
ponds dyed red with blood.

The night sky
bursting, astonishing
Depression-era boys
who've never seen
fireworks.

SHELLBACK

I wouldn't expect men on their way home from war
to be bird-watching off the starboard
or stringing dewdrops.

Nor would I think they'd force a fellow sailor
to swallow a box of laxatives,
make him crawl through a week's worth
of ship's garbage, through teeming larvae
in equatorial heat, or make a man
who'd faced kamikazes kneel and kiss
their fungal toes, and as he does, shock him
with an electric rod until he passes out.

I wouldn't expect the captain
to look on and laugh from the conning tower.

This was the shellback ceremony—
Navy initiation for sailors crossing the equator
for the first time.

This is one shellback's daughter
trying to find that wiser self within
who can forgive these men,
for they've come from Okinawa
where they watched a buddy's skull
blow out of his head,
teeth still gripping his last cigarette.

PATTERNS

After Philip Levine's "Heaven"

If you were twenty-seven
and had been on a ship
in the South Pacific,
if you had been the target
of planes whose pilots
were determined to die
just to kill you, you might,
when you got home,
mow the lawn with your jaw
clenched, making patterns
in the green. You might
spend hours teaching a deaf dog
to talk, raise your children
tight-lipped, unable
to speak for the din of siren calls
to general quarters, crash
of planes on a metal deck.
You might think that holding it in
kept it from us, but we
could feel it. We could see
from the patterns in the green—
something was in there
and so it was
our war too.

POLAROID

In a shoebox of old photos—
        here's one of me.

I remember the day
        watching my face come into focus

smelling the pink stick
        my father slid over my image

to make it last
        all the way to now.

It's my eighth birthday.
        I'm in a new outfit from JC Penney.

I'm sitting on a pile of giftwrap,
        an open present,

my eyes big as a Keene doll's—
        tear-filled, reflecting

the hands holding the camera,
        the clenched jaw

warning me not to cry
        or I'll give you something

to cry about. I was happy
        at least he didn't tell me to smile.

PORTRAIT OF MY FATHER AS A DAD

The gin martini his think drink, Mom ices the shaker every night as he comes up the walk from work. Captain Puget's running the cartoons on KOMO—Felix the Cat and Chilly Willy. It's Friday. I'm seven. Waiting for fish sticks. *I'll break every bone in your body if you don't turn down that TV,* he says. I picture his hands busting me up, one bone at a time, as Gooney Bird crushes Chilly with a mallet. He drains his martini at the dinner table, tells me I have *a chokin' size neck,* words rising with the smoke of his Old Gold.

THE BELT

wrapped around wrist / whistle / snap flick / snake

tongue / on my big sister's white thigh /

her pedal pushers down / I'm under

the dining room table / watching / promise self

I'll never do anything wrong /

over now / she walks to her room /

head high / doesn't cry / he runs

the belt back through the loops /

head down / hurt worse

FORGIVE

doesn't mean I've forgotten,
that we've talked it out,
that it's all ok.

All these are separate.

I let memories I can't erase
rest in peace,
knowing no one is only
their sins.

THE SADDEST THING

It is a man's first trip to Cairo. He waits in a taxi outside the train station while his driver pays a boy who's been guarding his cab. Next to the taxi is a man with a donkey hooked to a cart. The man clucks and shakes the reins but the donkey won't move. The man takes out a whip and hits the donkey, softly at first, then hard. The donkey still won't move. Then the donkey's legs tremble and he falls down dead. The man in the taxi is my father. He tells me this is the saddest thing he has ever seen. Most people would be sad for the donkey. My father was sad for the man. *I'll never forget the look of pain on his face,* my father says. *Kneeling over his dead donkey, outside the busy train station, blaming himself.*

LEFT TO RIGHT

My father was five
        when the nun
        took the pencil
        out of his left hand
        and put it into his right.

He couldn't make
        the letters that way
        but had to try
        or he'd be failed.

He tells me about that nun
        every time I visit—
        not repeating himself
        the way old people do

but trying to get it all out,
        trying to convince himself
        he was innocent.

We will never know
        what it cost him.

THE STRING

I go to my father's room to take him to dinner and find him
face down on the floor. Thinking he's dead, I say, *Daddy?*

I think I'm at the end of my string, he says, so I call 911.
He wants me to pick him up but he's dead weight.

I call an aid for help and we get him into his chair
where she checks his vitals—okay.

EMTs come and check his vitals again—okay again—
but my father says, *Something's not right,*

so they slide him into their Cab-u-Lance,
a repurposed delivery van, to take him to the ER.

Lying on a rack where bread loaves were meant to be,
he watches me out the back window as I follow

in my rental car and I know he's thinking I'm following
too close but I'm afraid I might lose them—

lose him. He's ninety-six. He said *something's not right.*
Through the usual rain-fog, I see my father

in the window grinning at me. Shit-eating?
Embarrassed by all of this fuss? Just happy I'm here?

I smile back thinking how he called life
a *string,* how string ties things together, how at first

there's a whole life to unravel, and the more string
comes off, the closer you get to the heart,

where there's no surprise, nothing inside,
just the end of a string.

HORNY GOAT WEED

I'm cleaning the kitchenette of my father's studio
at the retirement villa where he's agreed to live out his days.

I'm dusting the pharmacopeia that keeps him alive
when I see the bottle of Horny Goat Weed.

In the bathroom, I type the name into my phone—
I read it's a remedy for erectile dysfunction. *Take two*

prior to activity. If desired take up to three.
My father's ninety-six. My mother's been dead for years.

When I come out of the bathroom, I see he's thrown
the Horny Goat Weed into the trash. Of course, I pretend

not to notice. When I get home, I take out all the self-help
books I've hidden under my bed. *Conquering Guilt, Hiding*

Shame, Looking for Love. I stack them in the refrigerator
for the next person needing milk to read.

IN MY FATHER'S HOUSE

Three-bean salad sweats in stainless steel tubs.
House of chicken cutlet, lime Jell-O, buttermilk biscuit.

Pete Fonk's chair is empty.
Stopped breathing last night in front of the TV.

I'm a frequent visitor here. Friend of the old folks.
Oxygen tank, emergency pull cord, Mylar balloons.
Happy Birthday.

There are 63 rooms in my father's house.
House of easy listening, warm shawl, game show.

Elementary school kids are marched in—
taping hand turkeys to steam table.
Next month, come a-caroling.

Let's hear it for the volunteers—
large-type library, bingo, sing-along.

I'm ready to go, Miriam Falhberg whispers in my ear.
I love Miriam—purple afghan, Swedish accent, shortbread.

Love my father, too—
Seahawks, recliner chair, brown scapular.

In praise of Vera Dahlquist, Room 23—
lifer at Scott's, TP line, COPD, still sneaking smokes.

Tip o' the hat to van ramps, Bible study, mall outing.
Ode to pill cup, flower arrangement, broken gait.

Let's give it up for adult diapers delivered to my father's door. *Consider the alternative,* he says. Deadpan. Humor.

Never thought he'd end up here.

THAT FINAL WISDOM

My father won't drink water.
After the Dixie cupful
they make him take
with his meds,
he's done for the day.
A visiting nurse,
seeing the viscous,
bourbon-color liquid
in the plastic portable urinal he keeps by the bed said,
Mr. O, you gotta drink or you're gonna die.

What he's not telling us is
it hurts to pee and he thinks if
nothing goes in, nothing
will have to come out.
The Buddha said,
Let all the flesh and blood of my body dry up.
I welcome it!
But I will not move until I attain that final wisdom.
My father's body thinks otherwise;
his urethra shrinks to the width of a pin.

Slams cold enlightenment.

BIKINI EXPRESS

When I visit my father he always says,
Let's go to Bob's and get a senior burger,
and on the way there we always pass
the bikini espresso shack where
the barista, sometimes in nothing but a thong,
is working her big silver Cimbali—
banging used grounds from the filters,
wiping milk foam off the rods.
My father always tells me to slow down
so he can get a good look at the barista
and I'm always surprised he doesn't mind
my knowing he wants to see.
Once we pass, he always tells me
what lane to get into, to swing wide
to avoid hitting the curb, and park
in the handicapped because, as always,
he's forgotten to bring his cane.
When our burgers arrive,
he always tells me the story of Hot Cups,
the bikini espresso shack that blew up.
It was a cold January morning.
The near-naked barista was firing up
the space heater that kept her tiny kiosk warm.
There was a flash.
The shack burst into flames.
The barista jumped out the window
but she didn't get out with her life.
Single mom, two kids—
that shack was going to be her salvation,
the obituary said.

My father and I finish our senior burgers,
figure the tip, get back on the road.

You never know about a person,
he always says as we pass the shack again.

DA VINCI THEATER

1.

8 AM, Everett, Washington. A cold surgical theater.
Attending nurse, a former garbage truck dispatcher
who lost her job to a computer, holds my father's hand.

In my next job I wanted to help people, she tells him.

To calm him, she reminisces about her days in refuse removal.
Statistics, timetables, Dumpster overflow reports—
the unsung machinations of waste management.

2.

Doctor, sitting at a console in next room, programs da Vinci,
a robot with elegant wrists, to reopen my father's urethra—
slice the tip and bore in the length of the blockage.
Screen in theater lights up. All systems go.

3.

Mission accomplished.
By a robot and a computer.
WTF.

4.

My father peeing without pain now
but too weak to get to the bathroom alone.
Leans on me.

As we make our way,
I want to stop,
put my arms around him, tell him

I love him but don't—
afraid it might embarrass him.

ODE TO STENOSIS

The highway
that runs
down
my father's spine
is getting
narrower,
so narrow
the signals
can't get through.
My brain's not
talking to
my muscles,
he says.
He can't lift
cup to lip,
can't grip
a grab bar
to take
a shower,
and I read
that to bite
into a sandwich
or watch a sunset
requires neuronal activity
so complex
and elaborate
we can't
conceive it
much less
understand it
as a repertory
of cells
firing.

My father's brain
may not be talking
to his muscles
but it's yakking
a shitstorm of
useless
worn out
no good
to a man who
built two houses,
shot a hole in one,
dodged a kamikaze.

GET THE BODY YOU WANT

Middle of the night, on your way to the bathroom,
you trip and fall on the wheelchair we insisted on
to keep you from falling. The heavy rollator
lands on top of you. When the aid comes
to escort you to breakfast, she finds you
on the floor—an animal in a sprung trap.

*

*Your father can no longer get from his bed to
the bathroom, can't use his hands to eat or drink,
doesn't have the muscle to cough. We can no
longer care for him here—he's agreed
to let us take him to the other side.*

*

We ask a friend who's a nurse to look in on you.
She tells us you're dreaming in purple.
That means they're ready to go, she says.

*

In three hours I'm at JFK. At 2 AM I'm standing
outside your room. It's Father's Day.
An aid is changing your disposable briefs,
telling a joke as he tucks in the tabs and presses
the Velcro. I listen at the door, loving the man
for trying to distract you from the humiliation.
Why did you come? you ask when you see me.

*

At 6 AM I find you in reception—a VIP lounge
of wheelchairs waiting for the flight to breakfast.
Your head flops forward, a wilted sunflower.
Without muscle to sniff or swallow, your mouth
and nose let drain what's left of your life.
I touch your shoulder. *Happy Father's Day*, I say.

I push you into the breakfast room. Your name
is on a tray of bacon and eggs. I put a bit of egg
in your mouth, but you can't get your jaw to chew,
your throat to swallow. *This isn't working*, you say,
and ask to go to bed. The TV in the corner
plays country. A placard on the screen says
Get the Body You Want.

THE HOYER

Getting my father
from his wheelchair into bed

takes two aids and the Hoyer—
a motorized lift with a sling.

Dignity stripped
by the strapping in,

he's deadpan
through the whole business.

The agile crane hums
as it lifts him, then sets him

down to rest.

SOMETHING SO WONDERFUL, SO TERRIBLE

My father has three and a half days to live
when he tells me he's always wanted to be a singer
but couldn't, he says, because he was *no good.*

He asks, *Could I sing for you now?*
Lying flat in his bed, he takes what's left
of his breath and sings a song he learned as a boy.

> *I don't want to play in your yard*
> *I don't like you anymore*
> *You'll be sorry when you see me*
> *Sliding down our cellar door*
> *You can't holler down our rain barrel*
> *You can't climb our apple tree*
> *I don't want to play in your yard*
> *If you won't be good to me*

Then he sings Tommy Dorsey's "Yours."
That was our song, he says, looking at my mother's picture.

DAY OF THE GIBLET

You told me to buy the chicken hearts.
Slimy puce bullets shrink-wrapped to a Styrofoam tray.
You, on your deathbed, and I'm thinking
about those giblets—how you gave me the week's
grocery money, saying I could keep what I didn't spend.
Chicken hearts, 12¢ a pound.
Mom and Mame gagged.
You and I chawed the rubbery ventricles
with élan, knowing I'd pocketed a fiver,
not succumbing to split breasts.
You taught me how to stretch a buck, drive a truck,
anchor a screw, win at gin rummy.
Yesterday they stopped the heart
medicine that keeps you alive.
The room is quiet—no wheeze
of machinery, no metronomic pump,
no clips, no pole, no aluminum scarecrow.
Just soft Montovani over the PA
playing the heart out.

ANY FOOL CAN

sit by her father's bed and talk
          about the old days, watch shallow

breaths, count blue boomerangs
          on a faded gown worn by the many

who've passed this way, but it takes
          a tender-hearted lover of self

to get out of her chair to catch a nap
          or grab a plate of food, and when

I walk to the cafeteria carrying my
          clipboard with Medicaid application

and notes for Washington State
          Human Services, I'm mistaken

for a social worker by a man in a wheelchair
          whose wife is dying down the hall.

He is crying and wants me to tell him
          what to do. I explain

I'm just the daughter of someone else
          who is dying. I want to tell him

I'm a fool, I'm tired, and what little
          I have left is for my father,

not your wife. I don't say it.
          We look at each other,

me with my clipboard appearing
    calm and officious

in the matter of everyone's death.

YAY

If a body isn't viable,
        it isn't insurable.

So my father must pretend
        to want to live

while trying to die.
        A physical therapist

comes every morning
        and asks him to wriggle

his toes. She's in on it too,
        knows there's no hope

but says she sees a sign
        of improvement

she can put in her report
        so insurance won't think

they're putting money
        on a dying proposition.

        *

Don't leave me, my father says.
        He asks for water

but can't drink. I drip water
        from a plastic spoon

onto his lips. It spills down
        his chin, onto his gown.

Get a dropper, he says,
        angry I've gotten him wet.

We don't do droppers,
        a passing nurse says.

I find a clean gown,
        soak a corner in water,

squeeze it slowly
        onto his lips.

Yay, he whispers.
        Yay.

BATTLE STAR

We were told to take out a battery that had been hitting our ships.
We had to find out where it was.
The captain took us past a stretch of beach—
close enough to be in range of their guns.
We taunted and teased the Japanese into attacking us.
We got what we wanted.
We were hit five times.
A round sang past my head and hit the other side.
Missed me by a few feet.
I had to walk through the hit to get back to my bunk.
The bodies had been taken up but there was a mess there—
bits of uniform and flesh, bone shards, shoe full of blood.
For this I earned a battle star.

My father gave me the star the day before he died—
like I deserved it.

COMFORT CARE

We loved your dad,
the social worker says
as though he were already dead, loud
as though I'm deaf.
She hands me a book:
Hard Choices for Loving People.
This has been so much help to so many, she says.
Get her out, my father says.

*

Today death decides
it won't come easy.
JDO screams.
His arms and legs flail.
Parts moving that hadn't moved in days.
Nerve pain brings dead limbs
back to life. Miracles.

*

My father begs
to be flipped.
I ring, then run,
for the aid
who's too busy.

I punch arrows
on the motorized bed
to move his legs an inch,
then two, worsening
the pain. He screams again.
I try and fail
to flip him myself.

*

Morphine begun,
JDO is no longer JDO—
his voice high, light,
trying to tell a joke
the priest told the men
at the church building fund
meeting in 1965.
It's clean, trust me, clean! he says.
I'd never heard my father say
trust me.

There was a game
between Notre Dame…and…

Notre Dame and…Notre Dame…
who was playing?
Bless me Father…
there was a game…
trust me…
clean…

*

My father is smaller now down
to what can't cast a shadow,
all insides—heart, bone, feelings.
All he's been told not to show.

*

The drug has taken my father's brain.
He whimpers, cries like a baby.
Skin cold. Skull pressing cheeks.
He last ate three days ago.
Will he die of starvation?

The industrial kitchen across the hall
chugs away at mashed potatoes
and chicken-fried steak.
I can't let him starve to death
with a kitchen this close.

It's okay to die, Daddy.
Why don't you let go?
Not yet, he says,
starving for one more hour.
He moans like a man shot
in a war movie.

SUMMER SOLSTICE

I lean over the rails of your bed
to hear any last words.
You ask me to hold your hand.

The patio outside your window
is planted with roses in full bloom.
A semicircle of wheelchairs
is parked around them,
occupants murmuring
of their beauty.

Today is the solstice—
when sun stops.

*

I've just gotten into bed
when they call to tell me
you've passed.

I run for your room,
pulling on clothes as I go,
thinking you might
need something.

*

Your body is still
warm when I arrive.
They've cranked down the bed
and taken your pillow to lay you flat.
The easy listening is off.
Your eyes have been closed.

An aid waits outside,
to clean you, she says.
I close the door hoping
it won't seem rude,
that she'll understand,
we need to talk.

THE LIVING ALWAYS LEAVE YOU, BUT
THE DEAD STAY WITH YOU FOREVER

I've been asleep most of my life,
walking naked through brambles
gnawing mold off of berries, remembering
Amazonian fishermen I once saw in a film
who cradled their catch in their arms,
held it close to their breasts, humming
soft tunes until the fish died, smiling as it
tried to escape, as gills grasped at air.
My father has been dead six months.
Even a popup blocker can't stop
time-to-reorder notices
for Men's Size M flannel pajamas,
a fresh pair of scuffs.
Have you forgotten something?

Notes

Shellback: In *Merriam-Webster Dictionary*, https://www.merriam-webster.com/dictionary/shellback. Accessed 17 Mar. 2020.

"Epilogue": "The Cremation of Sam McGee" by Robert Service, c. 1917

"Something So Wonderful, So Terrible": "I Don't Want to Play in Your Yard," lyrics by Philip Wingate, music by H.W. Petric, c. 1894

About the Author

PHOTO BY MARK BERGHASH

JEANNE-MARIE OSTERMAN is the author of *There's a Hum* (Finishing Line Press). Her poems have appeared in *Borderlands*, *Cathexis Northwest*, *45th Parallel Magazine*, *The Madison Review*, and elsewhere. A finalist for the 2018 Joy Harjo Poetry Award and 2017 Levis Prize in Poetry, she lives in New York City where she is poetry editor for *Cagibi*, a journal of prose and poetry.

Paloma Press

MARCELINA by Jean Venua

SHIELD THE JOYOUS by Christopher X. Shade (2020)

PAGPAG: The Dictator's Aftermath in the Diaspora by Eileen R. Tabios (2020)

GLIMPSES: A Poetic Memoir (Through the MDR Generator) by Leny Mendoza Strobel (2019)

ELSEWHEN: PIECES by Robert Cowan (2019)

DIASPORA: VOLUME L by Ivy Alvarez (2019)

THE GOOD MOTHER OF MARSEILLE by Christopher X. Shade (2019)

THE GREAT AMERICAN NOVEL by Eileen R. Tabios (2019)

HAY(NA)KU 15: A Commemorative 15th Year Anniversary Anthology. Edited by Eileen R. Tabios (2018)

HUMANITY, An Anthology, Volume 1. Edited by Eileen R. Tabios (2018)

ONE, TWO, THREE: SELECTED HAY(NA)KU POEMS by Eileen R. Tabios (2018)

CLOSE APART by Robert Cowan (2018)

PEMINOLOGY by Melinda Luisa de Jesus (2018)

MY BEAUTY IS AN OCCUPIABLE SPACE by Anne Gorrick & John Bloomberg-Rissman (2018)

HUMORS by Joel Chace (2018)

ANNE WITH AN E & ME by Wesley St. Jo (2018)

AFTER IRMA AFTER HARVEY by Ivy Alvarez, Mary Kasimor, Agnes Marton, Lisa Suguitan Melnick & Eileen R. Tabios (2017)

MARAWI by Albert E. Alejo & Eileen R. Tabios (2017)

MANHATTAN: AN ARCHAEOLOGY by Eileen R. Tabios (2017)

BLUE by Wesley St. Jo & Reme Grefalda (2017)

palomapress.net